FORENSIC Investigations

BIG BANGS

Looking at Explosions and Crashes

Leela Burnscott

Smart Apple Media

This edition first published in 2010 in the United States of America by Smart Apple Media. All rights reserved.
No part of this book may be reproduced in any form or by any means without written permission from the publisher.

Smart Apple Media
P.O. Box 3263
Mankato, MN 56002

First published in 2009 by
MACMILLAN EDUCATION AUSTRALIA PTY LTD
15–19 Claremont Street, South Yarra 3141

Visit our website at www.macmillan.com.au or go directly to www.macmillanlibrary.com.au

Associated companies and representatives throughout the world.

Library of Congress Cataloging-in-Publication Data

Burnscott, Leela.
    Big bangs: looking at explosions and crashes / Leela Burnscott.
        p. cm. — (Forensic investigations)
    Includes index.
    ISBN 978-1-59920-457-4 (hardcover)
    1. Forensic sciences—Juvenile literature. 2. Criminal investigation—Juvenile literature. 3. Fires—Juvenile literature.
    4. Explosions—Juvenile literature. I. Title.
    HV8073.8.B864 2010
    363.25—dc22

                                                                            2009000382

Edited by Georgina Garner
Text and cover design by Cristina Neri, Canary Graphic Design
Page layout by Raul Diche
Photo research by Sarah Johnson
Illustrations on pp. 23, 25 and 27 by Alan Laver, Shelly Communications. Illustration on p. 24 by Jeff Lang.

Printed in the United States

Acknowledgments
The author and the publisher are grateful to the following for permission to reproduce copyright material:

Front cover photograph: A crash investigation team examines a damaged car and crash scene, by iStockphoto/Greg Nicholas

Background images used throughout pages: fingerprint courtesy of iStockphoto/James Steidl; tweezers courtesy of iStockphoto/
Mitar Holod; forensic investigation kit courtesy of iStockphoto/Brandon Alms.

Images courtesy of: Image copyright © Accident Research Centre, Monash University, **17** (top); © Department of Defence, **22**,
30 (middle left); Getty Images/Alex Wong, **14**; Getty Images/DAN TREVAN/AFP, **4**; Getty Images/Edy Purnomo, **5**; Getty Images/
Garry Williams, **17** (bottom); Getty Images/ODD ANDERSEN/AFP, **15**; iStockphoto, **29**; iStockphoto/Florea Marius Catalin,
21; iStockphoto/Greg Nicholas, **18**, **30** (bottom left); iStockphoto/Joe Gough, **8** (top); iStockphoto/Mel Stoutsenberger, **12**;
iStockphoto/Nick Free, **7**; iStockphoto/Paul Cowan, **8** (bottom); iStockphoto/Ryan Ruffatti, **20**; iStockphoto/Sascha Dunkhorst, **28**;
iStockphoto/Scott Leman, **30** (top left); Newspix, **11**; Jim Varney/Science Photo Library/Photolibrary, **9**, **26**; Philippe Psaila/Science
Photo Library/Photolibrary, **21** (bottom); Shutterstock/Greg Randles, **16**; Shutterstock/Maksym Gorpenyuk, **6**; Shutterstock/Teodor
Ostojic, **10**; Image copyright © Victorian Institute of Forensic Medicine, **19**, **30** (top and middle right).

The publisher advises that the names in the case study on pages 28–9 have been changed.

While every care has been taken to trace and acknowledge copyright, the publisher tenders their apologies for any accidental
infringement where copyright has proved untraceable. Where the attempt has been unsuccessful, the publisher welcomes
information that would redress the situation.

Contents

GLOSSARY WORDS

When a word is printed in **bold**, you can look up its meaning in the Glossary on page 31.

Science in the Court!

Forensic science is the use of scientific knowledge and techniques within the legal system, particularly in the investigation of crime. Forensic science can:

- determine if an **incident** resulted from an accident, natural causes, or a criminal act
- identify those involved in the incident
- identify and find those people responsible for the incident
- make sure that the innocent are not wrongly convicted

The term "forensic science" is quite misleading because it suggests only one type of science is involved. This is certainly not the case. Forensic investigations can involve virtually every field of science and technology, from electronics to psychology.

Forensic investigations require the skills of specially trained police, scientists, doctors, engineers, and other professionals. These investigators examine all types of evidence, from bloodstains to weapons and from bugs to computers. The greater the pool of evidence against an accused person, the greater the chance of a conviction.

A forensic expert presents crime scene photographs during a trial.

Big Bangs

Whenever there is an unexpected big bang, you can be sure that a forensic investigation will follow. Fires, explosions, shootings, and crashes cause the biggest bangs and their investigation can be the most time-consuming forensic investigations of all. There are often no quick results, just lots of chemistry, physics, and logical thinking.

The main aims of these types of forensic investigations are to discover:
- how an incident occurred
- who was involved
- if any laws were broken

Not all big bangs are deliberate. A big bang could be the result of an accident or **negligence**. In many cases, the kind of negligence that causes an explosion is a criminal act.

Fires

Each year, fires claim many lives and destroy much property and large areas of land. All fires need to be investigated to determine if they were the result of an accident, negligence, or arson. Arson is a crime. It is the deliberate lighting of a fire with the **intent** to do harm or make a false insurance claim. Some fires are started accidentally and are not criminal acts. Others are started through negligence, but only some negligence cases are classed as crimes.

The health and safety of the forensic investigators called to a fire scene always come before the needs of the investigation. No one should enter the fire scene until it is totally safe to do so. If a building is badly damaged by fire, parts of it may have to be knocked down before it is safe to enter. This, of course, can sometimes destroy valuable evidence and **contaminate** the scene.

Investigators examine a fire-damaged building to check if it is safe to enter.

DID YOU KNOW?

All forensic fire investigations are called arson investigations, even if it is eventually found that the fire was an accident.

How a Fire Started

Arson investigators include police and firefighters. They try to determine what caused a fire, and whether this was due to intentional, accidental, or negligent actions. Where arson looks likely, police look for a **motive** for someone starting the fire. The arson investigators concentrate on working out what fueled the fire, what the **ignition mechanism** was, and where the fire started.

Fire has caused extensive damage to this kitchen.

Fuels

A fuel is anything that feeds a fire. A fuel may be oil, gas, clothing, paper, wood, or other plant material. Accelerants are highly flammable fuels that increase the intensity and speed of a fire, such as gasoline and kerosene. When accelerants are present at a fire scene, this often indicates **foul play**.

How quickly a fire takes hold and how destructive it is depends on the type and amount of fuel at the scene. The more fuel and the more flammable the fuel is, the greater the fire.

Ignition Mechanisms

Fire investigators search fire scenes carefully, looking for possible ignition mechanisms. Fires are started by electrical, mechanical, or chemical mechanisms.

Electrical mechanisms that may cause fires are:

- lightning strikes
- power surges
- static electricity

Mechanical mechanisms are:

- **friction**
- leaking pipelines carrying flammable material
- bomb ignition devices
- the striking of a match

Chemical mechanisms are:

- fuels and accelerants
- gases

The law states that flammable liquids and gases must be clearly marked.

Chemical drums, such as this gasoline drum, may be the ignition mechanism of a fire.

Where the Fire Started

Knowing where a fire started sheds light on how and why it started. To find a fire's origin, investigators look for signs of upwards burning. When a flammable substance ignites, the flames shoot immediately upwards then spread outwards. Investigators also look for signs of the most intense burning. Fire tends to burn longer and stronger at its starting point.

Luckily for arson investigators, fires generally behave in similar ways. Investigators must also take into account wind direction and strength, the amount and type of fuel present, and the presence of shafts or stairwells, because these things alter fire behavior.

Forensic investigators search the remains of a burnt-out car to determine the cause of the explosion.

CASE NOTE

If a person claims that a fire in their home resulted from a cooking accident, arson investigators look for certain things. If more than one fire origin site is found, this indicates that the owner is lying and that the fire may have been deliberately lit. If only one fire site is detected and this is near the gas stove, then the owner may be telling the truth.

Explosions

Explosions make some of the loudest and biggest bangs. They make lots of mess by shooting **debris** over great distances. They also provide and destroy a great deal of evidence.

Like fires, explosions can be caused by an accident, negligence, or an intentional act. The three most common **triggers** for explosions are:

- fires
- crashes
- explosive devices

DID YOU KNOW?

A build-up of gases is what causes a carbonated drink to spurt out of a can that has been shaken up. It is also what causes the popping noise when a cork is removed from a bottle of champagne.

How Explosions Occur

An explosion occurs when pressure builds up within an enclosed object and is then suddenly released. When the explosive material in a bomb is ignited, it produces more and more gases, putting more and more pressure on the bomb casing. Eventually, the pressure of this build-up of gases gets too much for the casing, and the bomb and all its contents explode outward.

A bomb caused the explosion that damaged this apartment building.

A parcel bomb caused an explosion and a small fire in the office of the Australian National Crime Authority.

Fires and Explosions

Fires can cause an explosion or they can be the result of an explosion. Arson investigators try to determine whether the fire or the explosion happened first.

When a bomb explodes, it may cause a fire. The bomb's contents are forced outwards at great speeds, generating friction. This friction can ignite fires, causing more devastation.

Explosions caused by fires are usually accidental and not the result of foul play. Drums of chemicals stored in a factory may explode due to the heat of a fire that started accidentally in another part of the factory.

CASE NOTE

On March 2, 1994, Detective Sergeant Geoffrey Bowen from the Australian National Crime Authority opened a parcel delivered to his office. It was not a normal parcel. It was a parcel bomb. Bowen was killed and Peter Wallis, a lawyer who was also in the office, was blinded in one eye. The bomb caused an office fire and Wallis also received extensive burns.

Investigators determine if a car fire was caused by an explosive device, an electrical fault, or a crash.

Crashes and Explosions

When a vehicle crashes, its fuel tank can be badly damaged. If fuel leaks from the tank and comes into contact with the hot engine or radiator, it may ignite. The fire may then follow the fuel trail back to the gas tank, where it could cause the tank to explode.

Explosive Devices

Bombs, dynamite, and hand grenades are all types of explosive devices. Explosives are designed to generate large-scale destruction very quickly.

Explosive devices have been used both legally and illegally for thousands of years. Explosives such as dynamite are used to blast holes in the earth for mining, damming and road-building, and to demolish old buildings. Military agencies across the world use bombs and explosive devices during wars.

Homemade bombs may be used by terrorist organizations, in domestic disputes, in feuds, and in insurance fraud cases.

Gathering Evidence

Arson investigators, **ballistics experts**, and bomb experts are some of the forensic investigators who investigate explosions. They often have to search extremely large areas and sift through countless piles of evidence. They also deal with vital evidence that can be as big as the hull, or body, of a ship or as small as a tiny metal spring.

These forensic investigators analyze all the evidence to determine:

- what caused the explosion, such as a gasoline bomb, a letter bomb, dynamite, a gas leak, or a chemical fire
- the site of the explosion, such as the room in which the explosion occurred

When an explosive device has been used, investigators need to discover where the device was, such as outside or inside a building, and how it got there. A device could have been hidden at a scene, delivered by mail, or thrown through a window.

Firemen put out a fire and make the scene safe so investigators can start work.

Cause of the Explosion

Finding the cause of an explosion is often the hardest part of an investigation. When both a fire and an explosion have occurred, investigators need to work out if the explosion caused the fire or if the fire caused the explosion. They also need to work out if the fire was deliberately or accidentally lit.

Determining if the fire was the result of the explosion or the cause of it can be extremely difficult, especially when the target has a large amount of damage.

To find the cause of the explosion, forensic investigators look for:

- traces of chemicals or fuels that may have been used to make a bomb
- signs of electrical or mechanical faults that may have ignited a fire that caused an explosion
- shrapnel, such as pieces of metal, springs, or ignition devices, that could have been part of a bomb

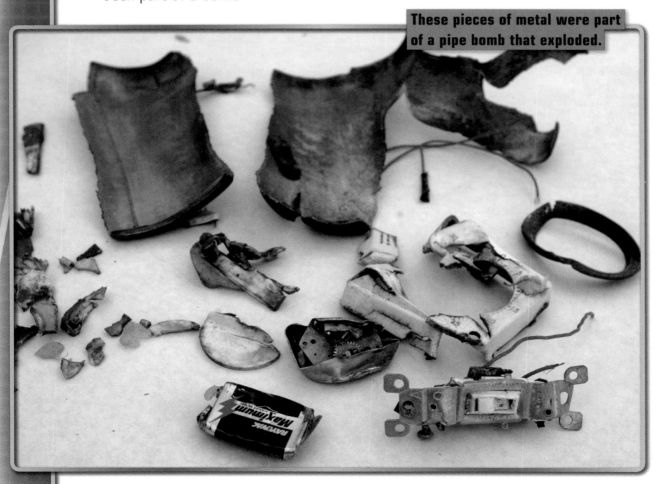

These pieces of metal were part of a pipe bomb that exploded.

Explosion Site

Finding the site of an explosion is similar to finding where a fire started. Investigators look for the area with the most damage.

Finding Explosive Devices

To discover how and where an explosive device was planted, examiners must look closely at the damaged site or target. In the case of the bombing of a ship's hull, experts will examine the metal around the hole in the hull to discover the direction the force came from. If the metal is bent outwards, the explosive device was most likely inside the ship. If the metal is bent inwards, the explosive device may have been attached to the outside and the force of the explosion pushed the metal inwards. In a similar way, the location of broken glass after a building explosion can help determine if the bomb was planted inside or outside the building.

Investigators also look for traces of tapes or wires stuck to an object. This could be from tape or wire used to attach an explosive device to a desk or to the undercarriage of a car.

Crashes

Whether they involve cars, trucks, airplanes, ships, trains, trams, or buses, crashes are unfortunately common events. Only those crashes that claim a life, cause serious injury or damage, or look suspicious are investigated by forensic experts.

How a Crash Occurred

Crash investigators are specialists in the fields of engineering or physics. They use their skills to examine evidence and work out how a crash happened.

Some of the most common causes of crashes are:

- driver error or lack of experience
- driver fatigue or tiredness
- mechanical faults
- poorly maintained vehicles
- alcohol or drugs
- speed
- driver distraction

Crashes also happen when:

- one driver deliberately drives into another or forces them off the road
- drivers deliberately break road rules
- something or someone unexpectedly runs out in front of a driver or falls in front of a vehicle, or a vehicle in front stops suddenly

Investigators must examine the wreckage of a plane piece by piece to work out what caused the plane to crash.

Examining a Vehicle

Examining a vehicle is a critical step in an investigation. Investigators must be on the lookout for:

- damage as a result of the accident, which can help indicate the speed and direction of impact
- pre-existing damage or faults that could explain the cause of the accident
- signs of deliberate **tampering** with the vehicle, which could be the cause of the accident and indicate foul play
- **trace evidence**, such as paint markings or flakes, which indicates that a second vehicle was involved

A crashed car is examined by two crash investigators.

FLIGHT RECORDER DO NOT OPEN

A flight recorder is often found in the carriage of a cargo plane.

CASE NOTE

Black boxes are almost indestructible audio-recording devices that are installed in the cockpits of all airplanes and some trains and ships. A black box helps investigators piece together what happened before a crash. If a plane crashed because the pilot was shot, the noise of the shooting would be recorded by the black box. If the crash was due to engine failure, the conversations of the pilots as they tried to deal with the situation would be recorded.

Examining a Crash Scene

Examining a crash scene involves looking for evidence such as skid marks, debris, and signs of alcohol or drugs. This evidence can help investigators determine how and why a crash happened.

A crash investigation team examines a damaged car and the crash scene.

Skid marks indicate speed, direction, braking patterns, and sometimes the intent of the impact.

Debris from the vehicle or vehicles indicates the speed and force of impact as well as providing information on the types of vehicles involved.

Fallen trees or branches across the road indicate the cause of the accident.

Signs of animals are another indication of the cause of the crash.

Rocks or bottles on the road could have been thrown at the vehicle, causing the accident.

Signs of alcohol or drugs in the car or on the driver are other indications of the cause.

The skids marks indicate that the vehicle swerved from one side of the road to the other.

Skid Marks

A skid mark is the mark a tire leaves when it rubs on the road after a driver suddenly applies the brakes. Forensic investigators analyze the length, width, and direction of skid marks to discover:

- the speed a vehicle was traveling
- if a vehicle braked before or after a crash
- if a vehicle swerved or was forced off the road

CASE NOTE

Finding no skid marks at a scene means something, too. This could mean that the vehicle did not brake at all because:
- the driver deliberately made impact and drove on
- the driver did not notice that they had hit someone or something and drove on

Long skid marks show that a vehicle was traveling at high speeds, because it takes longer to come to a complete stop when traveling fast. Skid marks found only after the point of impact, where a car hit another vehicle, indicate that the driver did not notice the other vehicle until they had hit it or that the driver deliberately crashed into the vehicle before braking.

Firearms

Firearms include rifles, pistols, and other guns. Firearms are responsible for thousands of injuries and deaths around the world each year. In most countries, all shootings are investigated by specially trained forensic officers, who determine if a shooting was deliberate or accidental.

Bullets and Guns

Bullets are small parcels of gunpowder packed tightly into a metal casing, called a cartridge case or shell. When a gun's trigger is pulled, a bullet is forced out of the gun. This pressure causes the sound of the gunshot and in most cases, the pressure causes the cartridge case to separate from the rest of the bullet.

Different types of guns have different firing mechanisms. In some guns, pulling the trigger sets off a spark that ignites the gunpowder, causing it to explode. In other guns, it releases a jet of high-pressure air that pushes the bullet out of the gun, or it releases a tightly coiled spring that snaps and forces the bullet forward.

Two cartridge cases at a crime scene are marked to be photographed as evidence.

DID YOU KNOW?

About 66 percent of all murders in the United States are committed with firearms. In Australia, less than 16 percent of murders involve firearms.

Ballistics Investigations

The study of firearms and shootings is called ballistics. Ballistics investigations involve three steps.

The first step is to discover the type of gun fired. This involves examining bullets, cartridge cases, and bullet holes found at the scene. If investigators are lucky, they will find a whole bullet. Most often, only bullet fragments are recovered.

The second step is to find the exact gun that was fired. To do this, the **impressions** left on the fired bullets and cartridge cases are examined. These impressions can be compared to test bullets fired from a suspect gun.

The third step is to determine how the shooting occurred. Was it accidental or deliberate? Was the target shot at close range or from far away? To answer these questions, the angle and height of the bullet holes, the damage caused, and the location of the victim and any cartridge cases need to be considered.

Impressions are left on the outside of a bullet when it is fired from a gun.

Two cartridge cases are compared side by side to check if the impressions on them match.

A ballistics expert test-fires a rifle in a special shooting range.

Identifying the Type of Gun Fired

Many different types of guns are produced today. Fortunately for ballistic experts, each gun type can use only a few types of bullets. Bullets differ in size, shape, weight, chemical composition, and cartridge type. Investigators use bullets found at a crime scene to work out what type of gun was fired.

Identifying the Exact Gun Fired

During the manufacturing process, the inside of each gun barrel is marked with a unique set of grooves, ridges, and scratches. As a bullet rushes down the gun barrel, these markings make impressions on the bullet. Similarly, when the trigger of a gun hits the base of the bullet, it leaves a unique mark on the cartridge case.

Ballistics experts use bullet markings to match a bullet to a gun. They test-fire any suspect weapons and compare these bullets and shells to ones found at the crime scene.

How a Shooting Occurred

To work out how a shooting happened and if a suspect is telling the truth, ballistics investigators look closely at bullet holes and bullet wounds.

Signs of gunpowder, soot, or burning around the edges of a bullet hole or wound indicate that a shooting was at close range. The closer the shooter is to the target, the more chance there is of **gunshot residue** hitting the target. Also, there is more chance that the bullet is still hot from being fired and burns the target as it hits.

By looking at bullet holes and the **trajectory** of the bullet, investigators can often determine where the shooter was in relation to the target. The trajectory can also tell investigators if the victim shot themselves or was shot by another person. Sometimes, murderers try to make a shooting look like a suicide or accidental self-shooting.

Gunshot residue when shooter is 3 inches (7.5 cm) from target

Gunshot residue when shooter is 12 inches (30 cm) from target

Gunshot residue when shooter is 18 inches (45 cm) from target

Blood Spatter

When a person is involved in an explosion, crash, shooting, or violent attack, there is often an explosion of blood. Specialist forensic biologists and **forensic pathologists** read this blood spatter and any bloodstain patterns to discover the details of the crime.

Bloodstain pattern analysis is useful in stabbings, shootings, and beatings. It can help reveal:

- the type of weapon used
- if there was a struggle
- where an incident occurred
- if a victim tried to escape
- where an attacker was

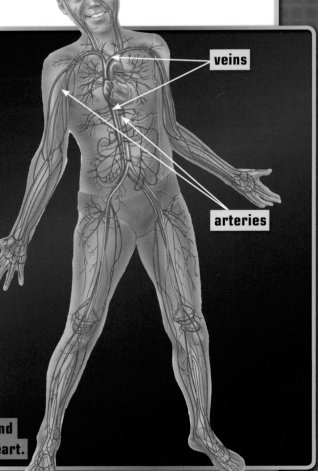

Under the Microscope

The heart pumps blood around the body through blood vessels called veins and arteries. The blood is under great pressure as it races along these blood vessels. If the skin and large blood vessels are broken or burst suddenly, blood spurts out. When one of the major arteries is damaged, blood will shoot up like a fountain and a victim can quickly bleed to death. Smaller wounds may result in just a trickle of blood.

veins

arteries

Veins carry blood to the heart and arteries carry blood from the heart.

Blood Drops

The shape and size of individual blood drops in blood spatter provide a great deal of information about a crime.

Perfectly round drops found on a flat surface indicate that a victim was:
- not moving when injured
- at a 90-degree angle to the surface, so not lying flat on the surface
- at a great height from the surface, so probably standing

Oval drops indicate that a victim was at a 60-degree angle from the surface, so probably slightly bent over.

Elliptical drops are oval-shaped drops in which the drop's length is twice the width. Elliptical drops mean that the victim was at a 30-degree angle from the surface, possibly doubled over.

Tear-shaped drops indicate that a victim was moving. The tail or point of the drop points away from the direction the victim was moving. A highly distorted drop indicates that the victim was close to the surface.

Bloodstain Patterns

It is not just individual blood drops that are useful. The position, size, and number of blood drops can help investigators work out what happened. Smeared bloodstains on a surface can indicate movement and contact.

Shootings often produce a lot of blood spatter, because a bullet has a lot of force. A very violent attack can produce a great deal of blood, too.

CASE NOTE

When an attacker shoots a victim at close range, a mist of tiny drops of blood spatters back onto the attacker and their gun. This back-spatter evidence can link the attacker to the crime.

Bloodstain patterns are measured and analyzed by a blood spatter expert.

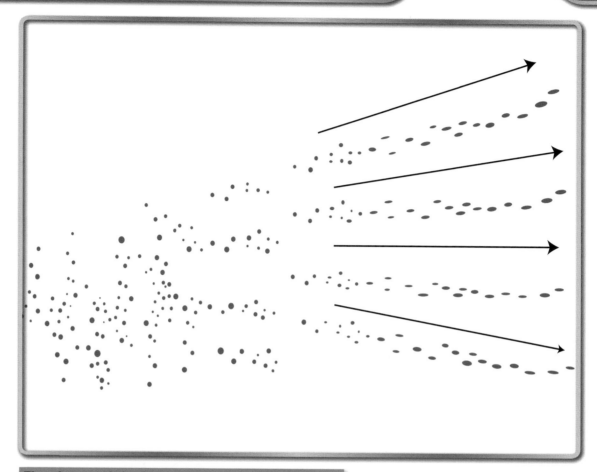

The shapes of the blood drops in a cast-off blood pattern tell a forensic investigator about a crime, such as where an offender was standing.

Cast-Off Blood Patterns

Blood spatter found on the ceiling or away from the main pools of blood is called cast-off blood. Cast-off blood is blood that is flung off an object such as a weapon.

Where cast-off blood ends up depends on the size and weight of the object and the force used to swing it. This determines the length, width, and height of the cast-off pattern.

Deadly Parcel

Background

Aimy Gregory lived with her two young children in New Zealand. The children's father, George, did not live with them. On this day, the children were with their father for the day, so Aimy decided to go out for the afternoon. She visited her friend Louise and then they went out shopping. They arrived back at Aimy's house at around 4 P.M.

The Crime

A neighbor saw Aimy and Louise arrive home. He watched as Aimy picked up a parcel that the postman had left on the doorstep. A few minutes later, there was a loud explosion. The neighbor ran over to Aimy's house and came across a bombsite. The entire side of the house, where the kitchen had been, had blown up. Aimy was dead and Louise was badly injured.

A small explosion damaged part of this house.

The police were immediately called in and they began their investigation. They had to work out if the explosion was due to an accident, such as a gas leak in the kitchen, or a deliberate bombing. By searching for the area with the most damage, the investigators were able to determine that the kitchen sink was where the explosion took place, so this was probably not a gas leak. They knew that this was probably a murder investigation.

The Evidence

Police set up a bomb reconstruction site. They worked out that four sticks of the explosive gelignite would cause the same amount of damage.

They carried out a grid search of the area up to 131 feet (40m) away from the house. Overall, 1,646 pieces of evidence were examined.

The parcel's packaging was found undamaged in another part of the house. By looking at the wear and stretching of the packaging's fibers, the experts predicted that it had covered a small box, which would exactly fit four sticks of gelignite. Fingerprints matching George's were later discovered on the packaging.

Many pieces of painted black chipboard were found all over the crime scene and even in the gutters of the neighbor's house. The investigators worked out that these were from the box that had held the gelignite. The paint from these pieces matched black paint found in George's garage.

Many pieces of metal were also found at the crime scene. They had been part of the bomb. It was discovered that some came from connectors used in Volkswagen cars. A box of Volkswagen spare parts, including connectors, was also found in George's garage.

By contacting local suppliers, the police were able to prove that George had bought four sticks of gelignite and some detonators earlier in the year.

George was charged and confessed to the bombing. He was sentenced to life in prison.

The explosion in this case study was caused by four sticks of gelignite.

Investigating the Investigators

Most forensic investigators are police members who have a science, engineering, or other relevant university degree. Outside experts are also involved. The following investigators are just some of the experts involved in the investigation of fires, explosions, shootings, and crashes.

Arson Investigators

Arson investigators are specially trained police, fire officers, or scientists who study fire behavior, accelerants, fuels, ignition sources, and all other aspects of fires.

Forensic Biologists

Forensic biologists are specialists who interpret bloodstain patterns, carry out blood typing, and analyze DNA.

Ballistics Experts

Ballistics experts are specially trained people who examine firearms, bullets, cartridge cases, and other projectiles. They are often the same officers who examine weapons and tool marks.

Forensic Pathologists

Forensic pathologists are medical doctors who specialize in carrying out autopsies. Their main role is to determine how, when, and where a person died, but they also examine wounds on surviving victims. Pathologists often examine bloodstain patterns at the crime scene.

Crash Investigators

Crash investigators are also called major collision investigators. Crash investigators are trained in engineering, mechanics, or other related fields. They examine skid marks, crash debris, and crashed vehicles to discover the causes of road accidents.

Glossary

ballistics experts   experts who study firearms, bullets, cartridge cases, and projectiles

contaminate   change or make impure by adding something

debris   scattered wreckage

forensic pathologists   medical doctors who specialize in carrying out autopsies

foul play   behavior that is against the law

friction   the force generated when two surfaces rub together

gunshot residue   tiny particles of gunpowder and other chemicals released from a bullet that has been fired

ignition mechanism   process by which something is caused to catch fire

impressions   marks, imprints, or prints made by the pressure of an object on a surface

incident   violent, dangerous, or criminal event

intent   aim, plan, or purpose

motive   reason for doing something

negligence   not taking proper care of something or someone

projectiles   objects propelled through the air

tampering   interfering with something so that it is damaged or changed

trace evidence   evidence that is present in very small amounts only

trajectory   path an object travels through air

triggers   things that cause something to happen

Index